Seahorses

Conservation and Care
Revised edition

Neil Garrick-Maidment

Photographers:

Linda Lewis
David Higgs
Francis Apesteguy
Sue Daly

Cover picture:

Short-Snouted Seahorse
(*Hippocampus hippocampus*)
Sue Daly

Contents

Foreword 4

What is a Seahorse? 5

Setting up the Tank 10

Feeding Seahorses 14

Breeding Seahorses 18

Seahorse Health 24

Seahorse Gallery 30

Seahorses of Great Britain
and Ireland 42

Glossary of Seahorse
Food 46

Index 48

*F*oreword

Mention the seahorse and everyone knows the kind of creature we are talking about.

Or do they? Most know what the seahorse looks like, conjuring up a mental cliché of a curious creature, half horse, half fish, swimming among glittering corals in clear, blue tropical seas. However, most of us would really struggle to recall anything else about these enchanting fish. This is excusable: until recently the seahorse has been an enigma, with very little known about its breeding requirements, diet or behaviour.

One certainty is that wild populations are under threat in a big way from exploitation in the medicine and trinket trades, and the popularity of the seahorse as an aquarium fish is only aggravating the problem. Until recently, keeping these fish has been a case of trial and error, most individuals sadly dying within a few weeks of being bought by well-meaning fish enthusiasts. This is mainly due to ignorance and bad advice, and the situation has been worsened by lack of literature describing the complications and difficulties peculiar to seahorse husbandry.

In this excellent book Neil Garrick-Maidment has at long last provided an accurate guide to these animals, combining an account of their natural history with his experience of seahorse culture in captivity. This book is a 'must' for anyone interested in the well-being of these fascinating fish, but especially to anyone thinking of embarking on seahorse keeping as a hobby.

Nick Baker
National Geographic and BBC

Dedication

To my wife Maxine, who has endured Seahorses
24 hours a day, and without whose support none of this
would have been possible. I love you!

Also to Mr Leslie Jackman who awakened in me the
interest I have today and inspired so many youngsters to
look beneath the surface of the sea and stare in wonder.

Neil Garrick-Maidment

What is a seahorse?

There is no doubt that a seahorse is a fish: it lives in water, breathes through gills and has a swim bladder. However, it also has some very strange and unusual features, the most striking of which is its tail. During the course of evolution, the seahorse's tail became much stronger, enabling it to live a more sedentary lifestyle amongst the weeds. The tail has no caudal fin and is long and very snake-like. It is prehensile, allowing the seahorse to grip onto eel grass, other weeds and any holdfast to prevent itself from being washed away by the strong currents and waves in the shallow weedy seas in which it lives. Some of the seahorse's ancestors, the pipefish, have prehensile tails but these are not as well adapted as the seahorse's.

As the tail evolved, the head was also undergoing a transformation. Instead of following the line of the body as in the pipefish, the head developed a neck, the only one of its kind amongst fish. Over a long period of time, it bent forward until, eventually, it allowed the snout to point downwards, giving the seahorse its classic horse's head. The snout has adapted to be long and thin, allowing the seahorse to probe into nooks and crannies after its prey. The seahorse eats small crustacea, such as shrimp, which it sucks up like a hoover. This suck is possible because the gills have adapted to concentrate the water through a small siphon in the top of each gill. The small size of the siphon creates a strong jet of water very similar to the siphon in a cuttlefish, which can jet away at high speeds when alarmed. The whole suction process is set off by a trigger-like arrangement which, when released, can be seen under the jaw of the feeding seahorse.

Surprisingly, seahorses are found in almost every ocean of the world, from the tropics to Tasmania, and as far north as the cold waters of the Atlantic. Their habitat is shallow, weedy areas, especially eel grass beds, although they are also found in short algal 'tufts", coral reefs, mangrove areas and even just in muddy, silt seabeds. Seahorses go into deeper water during the winter to escape the ferocity of the sea as waves cause chaos in the shallow habitats. Recent research has shown that some species only occupy deeper water areas such as the Pygmy Seahorse (*Hippocampus barbiganti*) that lives in the deep waters of Indonesia on Seafans.

Being sedentary has made the seahorse a poor swimmer. It relies on a small dorsal fin that beats between 30 and 70 times per second to propel it along, and two small pectoral fins either side of the head help stability and steering. Despite this it can move surprisingly quickly over short distances. Seahorses found in the cooler temperate waters tend to have bigger dorsal fins in proportion to their size than their tropical cousins. The reason for this is unknown but it might have something to do with having to cope with stronger currents or swimming more to look for food. Seahorse babies (fry) have much larger dorsal fins which help them in the early part of their life when they spend the first six to eight weeks swimming around amongst the plankton. As they grow the proportion changes and the dorsal fin appears to get smaller. One or two of the smaller seahorse species have fry that will sink to the seabed when born a great adaptation for survival.

Like the chameleon, the seahorse has the ability to change colour very quickly and match any surroundings in which it finds itself. Seahorses have even been known to go bright red to match debris floating in the sea.

One remarkable result of their evolution is that they are able to grow fleshy appendages *(cirri)* on their bodies, giving them a weed-like appearance. The Leafy and Weedy Seadragons of South-eastern Australia (close relatives of the seahorse) have taken this to extremes: having forgone the prehensile tail, they float around bearing the best resemblance to a piece of weed you can find other than a piece of weed.

As you can imagine, this ability causes chaos when scientists try to identify seahorses, as individuals of the same species can differ so greatly with these appendages and their colour-changing ability that they can and do look like a number of different species. The scientists are using DNA analysis to try and clear up this matter.

Probably the most famous aspect of seahorse biology is the male seahorse's ability to get pregnant and give birth to live young. This is a true pregnancy, unmatched by any other male in the animal kingdom. Being able to give birth to up to 1500 babies at a time and get pregnant again within 24 hours must make the male seahorse eligible for some sort of award. Even more remarkably, because the young are nurtured in the male's pouch they come out

Portrait of a seahorse *(Hippocampus ingens)*

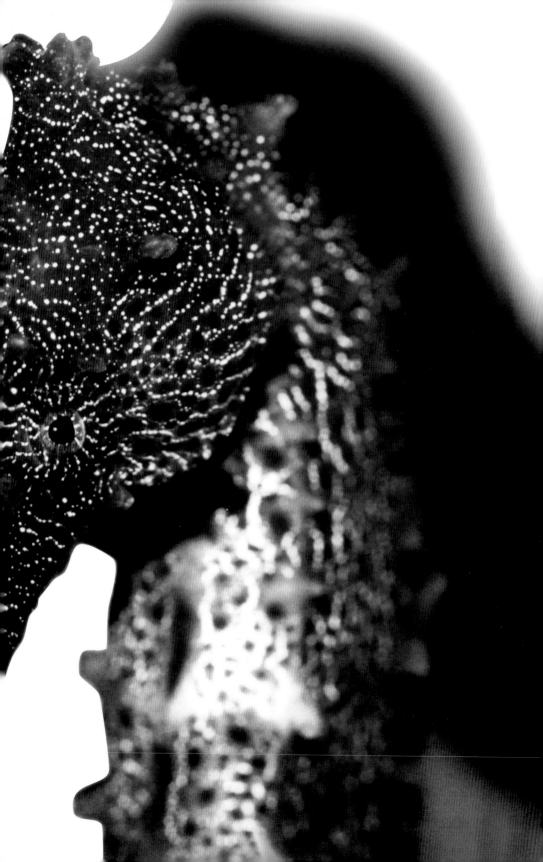

as perfectly-formed miniatures of the adults and are capable of feeding from the moment they are born. Their appetites are huge, each baby eating up to 3000 small shrimps per day.

The seahorse is able to look forwards and backwards at the same time. This allows it to keep an eye out both for its favourite prey, shrimps, and for

Yellow Pipefish (*Sygnathidae* species)

predators, but it must be confusing.

The body of the seahorse is made up of hard, external, bony plates that are fused together and covered over by a fleshy covering, unlike most other fish that have scales. Unfortunately, this exo-skeleton is the seahorse's downfall: when dead and dried out they still keep their unique shape. In this dried-out form they are sold as mementos of seaside visits and to the Chinese medicine trade in such large numbers that their future looks quite uncertain.

Seahorses are under threat in the wild from various directions. The Chinese medicine trade is by far the most devastating, claiming up to 30 million individuals per year (Dr A Vincent, 1995), being supplied by 65 different countries. They are used to 'cure' a number of different ailments; whether they work we do not know for sure, but we do know that if the collecting goes on at this rate then it will not be many years before the seahorse becomes a creature of the past.

The sale of seahorses as dried reminders of a seaside visit is also having a devastating effect on the seahorse population. One million individuals are collected

Weedy Seadragon (*Phyllopteryx taeniolatus*), by courtesy of *Express & Echo*

every year for this trade. Unfortunately many retailers believe that the seahorses are just washed up on the beaches and collected. This is not the case: they are deliberately taken from the sea and left to die under the boiling sun. A more painful death cannot be imagined.

Seahorses in ancient times

Seahorses have been known since ancient times, and almost mystical powers have been attributed to them by some cultures because of their unique way of life and, in particular, the male's ability to get pregnant and give birth.

In ancient times they were thought to be insects and were even listed alongside insects in some of the early books on Natural History. The word *Hippocampus* translates directly as 'Horse Caterpillar or monster'.

Stories of enormous seahorses dwelling beneath the ocean waves were probably what gave rise to legends of dragons. Some peoples believed that the white breaking waves were in fact 'Sea Horses' pulling Neptune's chariot through the oceans. The old manuscripts depicted seahorses as large, scaly, curly-tailed animals. Mariners returning from their journeys around the world would have told tales of the seahorse's strange lifestyle, the bony, scaly-looking body, the smoke-like particles emitted from the gills when it is eating, and the small fins either side of the head that look like wings, making the seahorse appear to be flying through the water. A stranger animal couldn't be imagined and, to a society that had little knowledge of the natural wonders in the world, this would certainly be an animal that conjured up magic and mystery.

Greater Tiger Tail (*Hippocampus comes*)

Setting up the tank

As with all marine tanks, you should take your time in setting it up, with plenty of forward planning and a lot of care. If you have never kept tropical marine fish before then it is a good idea to get experience with freshwater tropical fish before you progress to the inherently more difficult marine set-up.

Before starting the whole project make sure you have the budget to cover all expenses; just the electricity bill can be a major expense each quarter. Location and tank size are important considerations. When choosing a location bear in mind the weight. Each gallon of water weighs 4.5kg or 10lb - are the floorboards strong enough? Never place the tank in direct sunlight as the overheating and resultant algal blooms can both be fatal.

When considering the size of tank, do not think that just because they are sedentary seahorses only need a small tank. In the wild a female seahorse has a territory of about 1.4 square metres (15 square feet) and the male's territory is about 0.5 square metres (6 square feet). The only time they meet is first thing in the morning when they are doing their courtship display, so it is very important that they can get away from each other. Should you decide to keep more than one pair the extra room is vital but, be warned, do not overstock the tank, as stress is a big killer of seahorses. The bigger the tank, the more stable the water quality will be. So the rule should be: Think Big but Stock Thinly.

Your choice of water is very important. Despite thoughts to the contrary, it is possible to use natural seawater successfully in your tank. In fact, it is used by some of the major aquaria around the world. However, I must emphasise that you should be cautious when collecting natural seawater. Spend some time observing the wild fish in the area from which you intend to collect. If their behaviour is at all strange, or if there are no fish in the area, then choose another location. Needless to say, avoid areas that have obvious pollution, such as near industrial works or harbours and marinas.

After collecting your water, let it stand for at least 24 hours (if not 48) in an area that allows it to warm up to room temperature. If you do this, quite a large number of the harmful bacteria and bugs will die off. Keep the water aerated all the time by placing a simple airstone in the water. It is surprising what will colonise your tank after a period of time but always beware of creatures that might pose a problem. If

you do not have access to natural seawater, or prefer to use synthetic seawater, the quality is excellent these days, but be very careful when preparing the water. Take your time, check the balance of the water frequently and follow the instructions on the packet very closely. The main disadvantage with synthetic seawater is the cost: using natural seawater allows you to change the water very frequently. I change 10 to 20% of

The author collecting mysis shrimp.

the water once a week and when you start to breed seahorses you will need large quantities of water for frequent water changes.

Filtration is an area of contention amongst aquarists. Many people buy the latest gadget as soon as it appears on the market, regardless of whether they need it or understand what it does. Unless you are going for an invertebrate tank, the maxim 'keep it simple' should apply. The simpler it is, the less there is to go wrong. A good quality undergravel filter is essential; whether it is conventional or reversed flowing does not matter. You can either choose an air powered filter or power it with a powerhead. If you choose a powerhead, do not pick one that bleeds air into the tank as the air that is bleed in, is too fine and can cause sub-dermal problems. Air is vital to marine tanks so add an air pump and airstone to the tank to ensure they have enough air in the water making sure the air bubbles are quite large. Air is vital to marine tanks. Undergravel filters work on a biological

process, so the deeper the gravel the more area there is for the bacteria to do their job. The gravel should be a minimum of 3.25cm (1.25in) deep. If you have access to gravel from an established tank this will allow the bacteria to take hold more quickly, which will in turn 'mature' the tank. The undergravel filter is ideal for sorting out the bacteria, but an internal or external canister filter should be used to eliminate the larger particles. This will need to be cleaned at least once a week.

After installing your filters and part filling the tank you must decide on the 'furniture' for it. To do this, consider the lifestyle of the seahorse. In the wild, it lives in its own territory amongst the eel grass and other habitats, holding on to various plants with its tail, so you should give some consideration to its privacy when you are constructing the ideal seahorse environment. Start off by dividing up the tank, using large rocks as barriers for the seahorse to hide behind. You can then install small branches or twigs between the rocks. Be very careful as some wood, such as gorse, leaches poison into the water. Driftwood from the beach is ideal. Once you have the hard furnishings, turn your attention to the plant life. It is very important for seahorses to feel secure, so the tank must hold an abundance of plant life. Algaes such as *Caulerpa prolifera* are ideal because they are long-leaved like the eel grass and grow quickly and easily in the home aquarium by sending out runners across the bottom of the tank. Do not worry that, if there is a lot of weed in the tank, you will never see your seahorses. As long as they feel secure, they will be on show much more than you think.

Seahorses have very good eyesight. Their eyes work independently on either side of the head, a very good adaptation for hunting prey and keeping an eye out for predators at the same time. Flash photography, if done unsympathetically, will harm their eyes and so will very bright aquarium lights. You must strike a good balance between their eyesight and the needs of the algae. Life Glo tubes (a one-metre tube for a one-metre tank works well) are ideal for the job.

Once you have installed the algae and are happy with the set-up, fill the tank to the top with water, put in the heaters and allow it to settle for a couple of weeks. After this time, check the pH balance, specific gravity, nitrite and nitrate levels, and temperature of the water. You can get information from your local aquarist shop about the correct levels. Allow the tank to run for two more weeks and then do the readings again. If they are still within the recommended levels you can introduce your first pair of seahorses. Transfer them in a polythene bag containing water from the tank they have been living in up till now, and leave them in there until that water has reached the same temperature as the water in their new aquarium. Never

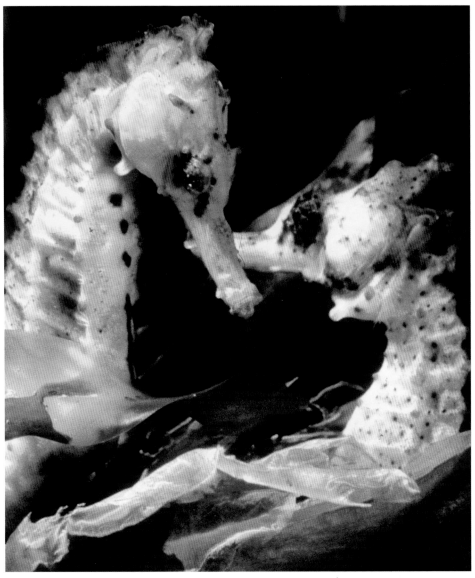

Yellow Kuda Seahorses (*Hippocampus kuda*)

introduce too many fish at once as it will upset the balance of the tank. Check the levels after a further week, and do this as a preventative measure once a week thereafter or if you suspect something is wrong in the tank.

If your tank provides the security that your seahorses need they will settle down very quickly and you will be more than pleased with their natural behaviour. You will be surprised how active healthy, secure seahorses are.

Feeding seahorses

By far the most important aspect of keeping seahorses is the feeding. Without good quality food, your seahorse will not live the years it should (the larger seahorses such as *Hippocampus kuda* should live up to seven years); it will probably be more like weeks. In an ideal situation live food should be given, such as mysis or river shrimp. Adult brine shrimp, unless they have been enriched (see page 16), are a poor quality food for seahorses and should only be used as a last resort. Seahorses hunt by sight and are often stimulated into feeding by movement, so the use of live foods is imperative, not only from the nutritional aspect but also for the behaviour enrichment of your seahorses' lives. If you give your seahorses natural things to do, they will behave more naturally and, in turn, have much better quality of life.

Should you live within a reasonable distance of the coast, then it is important that you take regular trips to the seaside. There is a good larder for the seahorses here and you should use it as often as possible. Countless small crustaceans that you can collect at low tide from rock pools and under rocks will be eaten with great relish by the seahorses. Rockhoppers *(Talitrus saltator)* and side swimmers *(Gammarus locusta)* are normally available in great numbers and will be consumed eagerly. There are also numerous small, brightly-coloured shrimp called Chameleon Shrimp *(Praunus flexuosus)* that can change their colour by eating a different colour of seaweed. Try experimenting with the food, and you will be surprised what seahorses eat.

It is also surprising how large a piece of food a seahorse can eat. Seahorses suck in food through their snouts, which expand if the prey is larger than the snout. Seahorses lack a chewing mechanism and have to disintegrate their food as they eat it. The long snout probes into nooks and crannies and the length has the added advantage of creating a more powerful suction for taking in food. The gills are sealed from the bottom to the top, with just a small opening at the top for the siphon. The

Kuda Seahorse (*Hippocampus kuda*) View of top of the head, showing siphon holes.

water is sucked in through the snout and concentrated through this siphon as it is expelled. There is also a mechanism similar to a trigger that is visible under the chin when the seahorse is feeding. When this trigger is set off it helps to accelerate the water through the siphon, again creating a more powerful suction. This powerful sucking action will actually disintegrate the food as it enters the seahorse's snout, allowing the seahorse to survive without having a chewing mechanism. Once the food has passed into the seahorse it enters the digestive tract, which is a short tube running down the front of the chest cavity. Unfortunately, because the food passes through such a short digestive system, it comes out only partly digested, which is why seahorses have to eat such large quantities each day. On average, an adult seahorse will eat between 30 to 50 mysis or other types of shrimp a day, and seahorse fry each eat a staggering 3000 pieces of food per day.

Should you not have access to live foods such as mysis or any of the others that I have described, you could try using the newly-born fry of mollies or guppies, although in my experience these are quite often ignored by even the most hungry of seahorses.

Training seahorses to eat dead food is a long and painstaking process but, if accomplished, is useful as a stand-by when live foods are not available. However, dead food should not be used as the sole form of nutrition. To train seahorses to eat dead food, begin by introducing small amounts of the liquid from defrosted mysis shrimp into the tank, being careful not to pollute the water. After a few days, drop small pieces of dead shrimp in front of their noses. At first, they will probably just watch it sink to the bottom or ignore it, but you must persevere. If you use this technique frequently each day, the seahorses will slowly start to take notice of it and pick at the odd piece. At this point, stop feeding live food and concentrate on giving dead food. You will notice the seahorses taking more and more, but do not allow them to get thin, as this will make them stop eating and, eventually, they will die. In a tank containing a number of seahorses, one will very often learn from the others about feeding on dead food, but you should always be aware of how much each individual is eating. A healthy seahorse is one who either bulges outward or is flat between each of the body ridges. If its shape is concave (going inwards) it is underweight and should be fattened up as quickly as possible. The only exception to this is when the female has passed her eggs to the male, in which case the lower three to four front ridges on her abdomen sink in, but within a few days her abdomen should fill out again as more eggs are produced and stored.

Those of you who do not have access to live mysis shrimp or similar should give very careful consideration to whether you should take on seahorses at all.

Hatching and enriching brine shrimp

When breeding seahorses you must make sure that you have a cheap and convenient form of food for the fry, and brine shrimp are just one choice. Even so, do not expect to raise 100% of each brood through using brine shrimp try just 10 or 20 fry first of all until you have more experience. The best food is live plankton but this is not available to most aquarists. To make sure you have a constant supply of brine shrimp, use four pots about a litre (1.8 pints) in size. Each pot must have a lid. Drill a hole through each lid, and put an airline with a diffusor on the end into each pot. Then place the pots in a warm location - the warmer it is the quicker the shrimp hatch.

To hatch out brine shrimp, fill the pot with seawater (synthetic or natural) and put a small teaspoon of shrimp eggs into the water. Place the lid on the pot with the diffusor in the water and leave in a warm, light area for 24 hours. Each pot should be started at 2 hour intervals. Once the shrimp have hatched, you then have to separate them from the egg cases. To do this, take off the lid, remove the diffusor from the water, and let the pot stand for about five minutes. After a while, you will see the eggs rise to the surface and the shrimp sink to the bottom. You can speed up this process by shining a light into the bottom of the pot. The shrimp are attracted to the light. Using a piece of airline pipe, siphon the shrimp from the bottom of the pot into another pot, being careful not to suck in the egg cases. Top up this pot with clean, fresh seawater. When starting off the next lot of eggs, clean out your first pot thoroughly and use new, clean, saltwater.

Newly hatched brine shrimp should be used within two hours of hatching, feeding just enough to be eaten before the next feed. This is ideal for Seahorse fry food for the first 4 to 6 weeks.

After this the shrimp will need to be enriched. Seahorses require quite high concentrations of algae in their diet, so buy any brand of algae tablets that dissolve into the water, such as algal wafers for algae eaters, and place one large tablet or two small ones into the pot. Some liquid algaes for marine fish are also available. It is best to use at least

Raising live shrimp for seahorses.

two different types of algae in the enrichment. You will also need to add a vitamin and mineral supplement. Experiment with the different algaes and vitamins available from your local aquarium shop. You will only learn what is best for your seahorses by trying as many as you can. Do not put too much into your pots or you will only pollute them. The shrimp should be allowed to enrich for at least 24 hours. Whilst the enriching process is going on, the airstone should be aerating the water.

After they have been enriched, sieve out the shrimp by pouring the contents of the pot through a very fine mesh. Wash the shrimp with clean water and then place them into the nursery tank with the seahorse fry. By staggering the setting up of the pots you will have brine shrimp available 24 hours a day. It is most important to keep your rearing pots very clean. When the fry have been feeding on enriched food for several weeks, start to train them on dead food as described above, when you are confident they are all feeding on dead food, only then, slowly wean them off the brine shrimp and onto the dead food.

It must be emphasised that good quality food is the basis for keeping and breeding seahorses. There is no short cut to giving them the correct, nutritionally-balanced diet they need.

Breeding seahorses

Seahorses have one of the most unusual breeding behaviours of any animal. The male gets pregnant. The seahorse is the only creature where the male has a true reversed pregnancy.

Some seahorses pair for life, Some seahorses pair for life, whereas others pair just for a season but they all live in their own territories for some or all of the time. The male's territory is about 0.5 square metres (6 square feet). The female's is 1.4 square metres (15 square feet), but it overlaps the male's. Bear this in mind when stocking your seahorse tank. Each morning the female visits the male's territory to reinforce their pair bonding with an elaborate courtship display. Once she has entered his territory, the male approaches her, changing to a lighter colour as he nears her. She will lighten her colour in response. The colours are often totally different from the normal colours. As they come together, the male constantly circles the female in a very tight spiral, keeping her corralled there while his colour almost glows with passion. The pair very often spiral around an object (often an exposed air lift tube in the tank), gripping loosely with their tails. This display can go on for up to an hour, with the occasional break during which they go back to their normal colours, changing back the moment the male starts the display again.

Unless the male has given birth during the early hours of the morning, the male and female separate at this point and go back to their territories until the next day. If he has, the display progresses further. The male starts to rise in the water, enticing the female to rise with him by doing contractions very similar to the ones he uses when giving birth. As he contracts, he sends a hormonal signal out into the water. His pouch is also flushed out during these contractions, making sure it is clean and ready to receive eggs. If the female is interested (it only takes her a few hours to prepare the eggs inside her) then she rises in the water with him. This rising together can happen continually for half an hour or so until the pair are positioned facing each other. At this point the female puts her ovipositor into the male, transferring the eggs in just a few seconds. In the smaller species, between 50 and 150 eggs can be transferred, but in the largest species such as the Big Bellied Seahorse (*Hippocampus abdominalis*) from South-east Australia, the male can take up to 1500 eggs. These males have extra membranes in their pouches, which provide more surface area into which the eggs can embed.

As soon as the eggs are in the male the seahorses break away from each other and the male sinks to the bottom of the tank. They change back to their normal colours and the mating is over. This is the last that the female has anything to do with the pregnancy and the only contact the male has with her is each morning during the reinforcement display.

After the male has sunk to the bottom, he self-fertilises the eggs inside the pouch, and at the same time does a movement very similar to a belly dancer, moving from side to side. This action helps to embed the eggs into the tissue of the pouch wall where they will be nurtured through a placental fluid during the gestation period. Inside the pouch they receive everything they need to grow into perfect miniature seahorses, from oxygen through to food. The pouch is an amazing organ. It is controlled by hormones, one of which is lactin, which in human females produces milk.

Gestation varies in time, depending on the size of the species.

The smaller species are pregnant for about 14 days, whereas the larger species such as the Big Bellied Seahorse can be pregnant for up to four weeks.

Giving birth can be a long and drawn-out process, with the contractions lasting up to 12 hours. As a result of pressure in the greatly distended pouch, some males release a few of their young several days before the main brood is born. These babies usually do not survive because invariably they are not fully formed. The actual birth is performed with a great flourish, and the tank fills with perfect miniature seahorses in just a matter of seconds. From this point on, the male has nothing more to do with the youngsters and is often seen lying exhausted on the bottom of the tank. However, he never seems to learn, because he will become pregnant again within a couple of days.

The young are totally on their own from the moment they are born but, having had the advantage of the security of the male's pouch, they are well equipped to go out into the big, wide world. Despite this advantage, in the wild less than one in a thousand will survive to maturity, mainly because of predation. From the moment of birth they start to feed, and their intake is enormous, each baby eating up to 3000 particles of food a day. This huge intake of food is the biggest problem for aquarists hoping to rear seahorse fry. The first 14 to 28 days of a seahorse's life are by far the most important because of the quality of the food it must take in.

As soon as the fry have been born, remove them to a glass-bottomed tank containing an air powered filter preferably an air driven sponge filter.

A pregnant seahorse displaying to his mate.

20

The author looking at a six-week-old Prickly Seahorse *(Hippocampus histrix)*.

Do not make the filter too powerful or they will be sucked into it. Transfer the fry with the water they were born in so that the change is not so stressful for them. The tank needs a good circulation of water, so use several air stones or an air bubble curtain spread out in the tank, again not too powerful. For the first week or so, you will not need anything for the fry to hold onto, but after this put in some artificial weed, which is easier to keep clean.

In the wild, seahorse fry spend the first two to three weeks in the plankton layer of the ocean, where they drift along in the currents. This is a dangerous time for them and most of them are eaten by other fish. There are one or two exceptions to this like the Knysna Seahorse *(Hippocampus capensis)* whose fry drop straight to the bottom and will need weed to hold onto from birth.

The most difficult part of rearing seahorse fry is getting the food right. The ideal food is zooplankton but the average aquarist does not have access to this. Another good source of food is rotifers but, if you intend to raise large numbers of seahorse fry, this is a very expensive and frustrating form of food, especially if it does not hatch out or multiply as quickly as it should. In the aquarium we use newly-hatched brine shrimp *(naupili)* as a convenient, but unfortunately poor quality, food. It does not seem possible to get high yields of seahorse fry with this food but it is easy and cheap for the average aquarist to use. Because it is such poor quality it has to be enriched. Not only does it give a better quality food but it allows you to get extra minerals and vitamins into the fry. (See page 16 for details about hatching and enriching brine shrimp.)

A hybrid seaponie against a human hand, showing the relative size.

To feed seahorse fry on brine shrimp, siphon the shrimp out of their pot through a very fine mesh and then wash them while they are still in the mesh by slowly pouring clean, fresh seawater over them. The shrimp can then be put into the seahorse fry's tank. Make sure that you do not put in more shrimp than will be cleared in 2 hours (you will learn this with experience). Siphon out the surplus shrimp before feeding the next batch. Feeding should take place every two hours to make sure that the shrimp contain the maximum amount of nutrition. Their nutritional value decreases as they swim about. You should leave the lighting on 24 hours a day for the first week, after which you can turn it off for longer and longer periods until you reach a normal day/night routine. With the exception of the seaponies (which survive on unenriched brine shrimp) you will lose at least 50% of your brood in the first 14 days, so it would be better to only select 10 to 20 of the strongest animals and concentrate on them, as your experience grows more can be selected with each successive brood.

The fry will survive quite happily for the first six to eight weeks on the brine shrimp, especially if the juice from frozen mysis is added at each feed (be careful of water quality) but at about week five you should start to change their diets. In an ideal set-up live mysis shrimp should be used at this point, but most aquarists do not live near a source for these and, even if they were available in your local fish shop, the cost would be prohibitive. For this reason, a technique of training the fry to feed on dead mysis shrimp should be used. During week one, scrape small particles of the frozen shrimp into the water, again being careful not to pollute. Slowly, over weeks six to eight, the fry will start to pick at these particles with more and more vigour. By weeks eight to ten they should be eating more and more of the frozen shrimp. At this point, reduce the brine shrimp in proportion. Bear in mind that seahorses need to feed all day and make allowances for this by feeding them several times a day. During the change from brine shrimp to frozen mysis shrimp you are bound to lose a few seahorses, as some will not be strong enough to cope with it.

A seahorse breeder should not consider him or herself successful until the seahorses are mature enough to start breeding. All keepers of animals whose numbers are depleted in the wild, whether they keep seahorses or elephants, have an obligation to breed their animals so that the depletion on the wild stock is kept to a minimum.

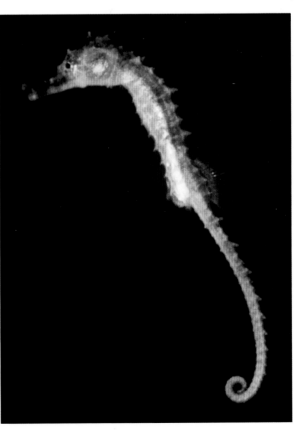

Many Branched Seahorse (Hippocampus ramulosus) at just a few weeks old.

Seahorse health

A healthy seahorse should have a good, strong colour, tiny glistening mucus deposits on the head and neck, and should be a good weight. You will learn how to judge a seahorse's weight by sight. Between the ridges of the body, the skin should either bulge outwards or be level; if it sinks inwards the seahorse is seriously underweight and should be offered more or better quality food. The only exception to this is that, when the females are carrying no eggs, the front four or five segments of the belly sink in.

If you keep your seahorses in good, healthy conditions then there is no reason why they should not live for years rather than the few weeks that appears to be common. If you keep your seahorse stress-free and in a clean environment you are half way to having a healthy, happy animal. I cannot stress enough that seahorses need to feel secure in their environment, so make sure that they have plenty of holdfast for their tails and plenty of algae in the tank so that they feel well hidden.

Because they eat a large quantity of live food it is essential to keep the tank spotlessly clean, removing surplus dead food and the faeces, which are quite large and can be quite oily. I would recommend that you change the seahorses' water more frequently than you would with other marine fish because of their diet. I change the water in all my tanks once a week (the main advantage of natural seawater) and therefore have very few problems with water quality.

More often than not diagnosing and treating diseases in seahorses can be a guessing game, as several are not known to science. The seahorse's physiology makes it an unusual creature to work with and we are still a long way from discovering exactly what affects it and how it reacts to varying stimuli. I have listed the most common recurring diseases below, but you are sure to come across unlisted diseases. Do not be frightened to experiment with treatments; you may help seahorse health in the long run.

A hybrid seahorse

Gas Bubble disease

This is a particularly frustrating disease. It is caused by stress and bacteria, and can affect seahorses in two different ways. The first affects the seahorse under the skin or internally. Gas Bubble disease can be detected quite easily and quickly if it is under the skin, because it shows up as transparent bubbles (hence the name),

usually starting at the tail. The probable reason is that the tail, always in contact with surfaces, is scraped or cut, allowing bacteria to enter the seahorse's system and start the infection. The other common place for the disease to show itself is on the snout, again because it is always in contact with the ground or against surfaces during feeding. Occasionally Gas Bubble disease starts in, or progresses to, the swim bladder, causing the animal to lose stability.

As far we know at present, there is no definite cure for this form of the disease, although you can help the seahorse in the short term if the bubbles are on the surface and you can get to them. You need to sterilise a very fine needle. Hold the seahorse just under the surface of the water and very carefully prick the bubbles with the needle. Be very careful not to go too deep or you will damage internal organs, ultimately leading to death. Never tear at the skin or use an unsuitable object like a cocktail stick, which will cause more problems than you had to start with. Once the bubbles have been expelled, you might have to massage the area with your finger to push out all the air. Once this has been done, you need to treat the wound with an anti-bacterial agent, which can be bought from a reputable fish shop. Put the seahorse in a separate tank while you are treating it and add the agent to the water. You will probably have to repeat this treatment over the next couple of days. Unfortunately, this is not a long-term cure, and you will probably lose your seahorse in the end.

This type of Gas Bubble disease is very virulent and destructive, and is often accompanied by fungus this often starts as small grey patches on the skin. If this is the case, then the skin will rot and, in extreme cases, the tail drops off or becomes totally useless. Rather than let it suffer, you should put the animal down by placing it in a pot of water in the freezer until it has passed away or ask your vet to put the animal down for you.

Fortunately, the second form of Gas Bubble disease can be cured. Male seahorses of all the species are very prone to gas bubbles in their pouches. The exact reason for this gaseous build-up is not entirely clear, but it is thought to be caused by bacteria. There are two possible causes; firstly, decaying matter in the pouch (dead eggs or embryos) or, secondly, an internal injury to the pouch. The consequence of the gaseous build-up is that the male loses control of his buoyancy and hangs upside down in the water, not being able to get down and anchor himself. This is a highly stressful situation for a Seahorse to be in. Should this go on for too long, he will starve to death as he is unable to feed properly.

Yellow Philippine seahorse (*Hippocampus sp*)

In the past, a number of what must have been very painful treatments have been tried for this problem, none of which was very successful in the long term. Treatments such as lancing the pouch with pins or needles, or opening the pouch to release the air with totally unsuitable instruments such as cocktail sticks, usually have one guaranteed result: death sooner or later.

The answer is to treat the cause of the problem as well as the problem itself. Hold the seahorse upright in your left hand, pushing the tail out of the way with your little finger and with the thumb and index finger either side of the pouch. With your right hand, insert the end of a fine, disposable pipette into the opening of the pouch. Do not force it in, just gently ease it in with a slight twisting of the pipette. This operation must be done whilst the seahorse is held under the water. As you gently massage the pouch up towards the opening the air will be expelled through the pipette. Once you are sure that the pouch is clear of air, use a fine nozzled hand spray to push a solution of warm water and Myaxin (or any anti-fungal solution) into the pipette, and flush the pouch clean. Once you are sure that the pouch has been thoroughly flushed through, remove the hand spray and the pipette, again very gently. You might have to repeat this procedure up to three times on three consecutive days.

I have had a 100% success rate with this technique, and the affected seahorses have gone on to breed quite successfully.

Fungus

Fungal diseases fall into two categories: slow affecting and curable, and very rapid and non-curable.

Slow affecting and curable: This form of fungus appears as a grey patch on the seahorse (not to be confused with a burn from the heater) and develops slowly. Remove the seahorse to a suitably-furnished isolation tank and add an anti-fungal agent to the water. Repeat the dosage each day until the fungus disappears. Make sure you change some of the water each day to guard against overdosing and the water becoming foul. When you are 100% certain the fungus has cleared up, reintroduce the seahorse into the tank with the others.

Very rapid and non-curable: The second fungus spreads very rapidly and is usually accompanied by extensive rotting in whichever part of the body it attacks. Again, isolate the seahorse and try an anti-fungal agent but, as far as I know, this form of fungal disease is not curable. If the fungus is causing the seahorse pain you must put the animal down rather than let it suffer.

Tiger Tail (*Hippocampus comes*)

Others

As well as the above, seahorses are prone to all other diseases affecting marine fish and should be treated in the same way.

They are a highly stressful fish and every effort should be made to keep stress to a minimum, provide good clean water, a good quality, preferably live food constantly and be careful in the choice of tank mates. They do not compete well with faster moving fish and can be harried by them. The most crucial aspect to keeping a seahorse healthy is by providing the correct environment, plenty of hiding areas, a good quantity of plant life and most importantly plenty of good sized holdfasts. A seahorse that is constantly swimming is a stressed seahorse if your seahorse is always on the move then try and work out why. By being stressed it will be prone to diseases and will live only a very short length of time.

Seahorse gallery

There are 30 to 40 species of seahorse and possibly as many sub-species, from almost every ocean of the world, including two from around the British coast. There is a huge confusion surrounding the naming of seahorses, with many species being called by the same name. *Hippocampus kuda* and *H histrix* are two commonly misused names, *kuda* in particular being applied to at least ten different species. Given their ability to change colour and add appendages to their skin it is very difficult to identify seahorses.

Different species

The nine species of seahorse shown on the following pages are the ones you are the most likely to encounter in an aquarium or fish shop.

Kuda Seahorse
(Hippocampus kuda)

Distribution: Western Atlantic, Gulf of Mexico, Caribbean and the Straits of Florida.

Size: up to 17.5cm (7in)

The Kuda Seahorse is one of several seahorses called by various common names, such as Common, Golden, Giant and Brown. The confusion comes from the mix-up over the different species and the fact that they can change colour.

Tiger Tail Seahorse
(Hippocampus comes)

Distribution: Indian Ocean, Bay of Bengal, Gulf of Thailand, Philippines and Java Sea.

Size: 10-12.5cm (4-5in)

This is one of the most striking seahorses, with its black and yellow banded tail. There are several sub-species of the Tiger Tail, possibly as many as eight. They are all slightly different: it might be length of snout, adult size or the basic colour, which varies from charcoal black to light grey. A difficult seahorse to keep the fry alive, because of there diminutive size.

Spiny Seahorse
(*Hippocampus guttulatus*)

Distribution: southern coast of the British Isles and up the west coast as far as Northern Scotland and then on up to the Shetland Isles, all around the Irish Coastline Possibly around Ireland as well. They are also found around the channel Islands on the continental coast and into the Mediterranean. Throughout this wide distribution it is possible that a number of sub-species are found.

Size: up to 17.5cm (7in)

This is the bigger of the two species inhabiting the waters around the British Isles. It is a very striking seahorse, with its 'mane' running along the top of its head and down its back. The colour varies from light grey to olive green. Although it is found only occasionally around the British Isles, there is definitely a sustainable population and with careful monitoring through The British Seahorse Survey, it is hoped this species will overcome all the pressures put on it by mankind in the form of pollution and habitat loss. See also page 42.

Prickly Seahorse (*Hippocampus histrix*)

Distribution: Indo-Pacific, around the Gulf of Thailand and South China Sea.

Size: up to 15cm (6in)

As its name suggests, the Prickly Seahorse is prickly to look at, which helps when it is camouflaging itself. The normal colour is light yellow but this differs with the various sub-species. The snout bands are very distinctive.

Short Snouted Seahorse
(Hippocampus hippocampus)

Distribution: All along the South
Coast of Britain and around the
Channel islands, along the
Western European coastline and
around the Mediterranean.
Size: maximum 15cm (6in)
This is one of two seahorses found
around Britain, from the easternmost tip of Kent to the west of
Cornwall and around the Channel
Isles. It is also found along the
European coastline right down into
the Mediterranean. It is not as
elaborate as *Hippocampus
guttulatus* but, nevertheless, is a
beautiful little seahorse. The
main difference between the
two is that this species lacks
a mane and is stockier.
See also page 42.

Golden Seaponie
(Seahorse)
(Hippocampus whitei)

Distribution: Eastern Australia

Size: up to 12.5cm (5in)

Very often this seahorse is bright yellow, hence the name Golden Seaponie. (Seahorse) 'Seaponie' is a term often used for the smaller members of the seahorse family Hippocampus. Like *H breviceps* (page 41), the Golden Seaponie very often has spiky appendages which make it look very weed-like.

Big Bellied Seahorse
(*Hippocampus abdominalis*)

Distribution: South-eastern Australia and Tasmania.

Size: biggest of all seahorses, growing up to 25cm (14in).

The Big Bellied Seahorse inhabits the cooler temperate waters of South-east Australia. Its name refers to the extra-large carrying capacity of the males. The pouch has extra membranes in it to increase the surface area for the youngsters in the pouch.

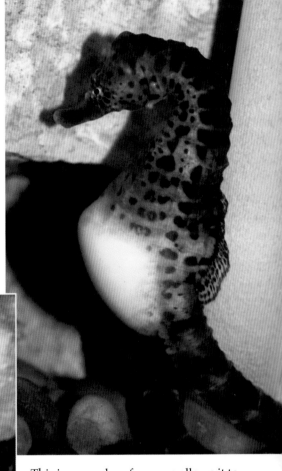

This increased surface area allows it to have up to 1500 youngsters at a time. As with all temperate seahorses, the dorsal fin is proportionally longer than in its warmer-water cousins, possibly to cope with stronger currents and the need to travel further to look for food.

Black Seaponie (*Hippocampus fuscus*)

Distribution: all around the Indian Ocean.

Size: up to 12.5cm (5in)

This is the most common of all the seaponies and, fortunately, is quite hardy although it is susceptible to fungal problems. It is usually black but, like all seahorses, can change to almost any colour under the sun. It has a very prominent crown on top of its head and tends to be quite smooth. If any seahorse can be suggested as a 'starter' species, this is probably the one, as it takes dead food quite readily, allowing the aquarist to feed it on dead mysis.

Knobby Seahorse
(Hippocampus breviceps)

Distribution: south eastern Australia and Tasmania.

Size: up to 10cm (4in)

A pretty seahorse, the Knobby looks like a Disney character with its out-of-proportion belly and turned-up snout. It is very often seen with spiky appendages on its head and back. When the male is pregnant, he looks as if he is going to explode because of the size of his pouch.

Seahorses of Great Britain

It comes as a great surprise to most people that there is one (let alone two!) species of seahorse around the coast of the British Isles. Many people believe that seahorses are tropical animals but, as we have seen in the previous chapter, there are several temperate species inhabiting cooler waters around the British Isles, off Tasmania and South-east Australia and even on the east coast of America.

The British seahorses have quite a wide distribution, from the easternmost point of Kent along the south coast to the Isles of Scilly, north to Bangor in Wales and on up to the Shetland Isles and around the Irish coastline. They are also found all around the Channel Islands.

Recent reports have shown there is also a possibility that they are also found in down the East coast of the British Isles. The two species look very different from each other. The Spiny Seahorse (*Hippocampus guttulatus*) is quite large, adults reaching 15-17.5cm (6-7in) from the tip of the tail to the crown on the head. The normal colours for *H. guttulatus* range from olive green to dark grey, with a sprinkling of glistening mucus deposits covering the head and top of the trunk, shining like little diamonds and providing a good indication that the seahorse is in good health. Along the crown of the head and down the back is a mane of prickly appendages *(cirri)*, each of which can be up to 1.25cm (0.5in) long. These appendages are much more distinct in the youngsters and seem to lessen as the seahorses age. The reason for the appendages is camouflage. With their dark colour and this elaborate mane the seahorses blend in so well with the weeds that even the most ardent searcher has trouble seeing them.

The other species around the British Isles is the Short Snouted Seahorse (*Hippocampus hippocampus*). The Channel Islands and the western tip of Kent are the most eastern part of their distribution, but they also extend along the coasts of

France, Belgium and Holland and down into the Mediterranean. They are slightly smaller than *H guttulatus*, lacking the appendages but of a similar colour. They also inhabit eel grass beds and algal tufts.

In 1994 The Seahorse Trust launched the British Seahorse Survey to try to find the exact distribution and population numbers of both these species. Any sightings are recorded on a survey sheet. Write to the following address, enclosing a stamped, addressed envelope, to obtain one:

The Seahorse Trust
The Seashore Centre
Tanners Road
Goodrington
Torbay
Devon TQ4 6LS

Many Branched Seahorse *(Hippocampus guttulatus)*

The details are being used to build up a more accurate picture of seahorse life so that they can be added to the Wildlife and Countryside Act and get the full protection that they need. Over the last 10 to 15 years, it has been noticed that sightings have reduced quite dramatically, and many researchers feel that this is an indication that the seahorses are slowly disappearing.

Keepers of seahorses are in something of a *Catch 22* situation. On the one hand, wild stocks of all species have been badly depleted so that it is not good to take any more from the wild. As will have been apparent, they are not the easiest of species to keep in captivity. On the other hand, careful husbandry of these fascinating creatures maintains endangered species in captivity and possibly provides a means of reinforcing their populations in the wild. If you are going to keep seahorses as pets, you must take great care to give them all their needs so that they live as healthy and long lives as they would in the wild. It is a responsibility that you should not undertake lightly. Remember, their future is in your hands.

Glossary of seahorse food

Brine shrimp

Adult brine shrimp are the food most usually recommended by pet shops as food for seahorses but, in the author's opinion, they should only be used when no other food is available, and then only for short periods. Although seahorses take them eagerly, the nutritional content is so low that, if this is the seahorses' only food for a long time, they will starve to death. (See page 16 for enriching brine shrimp.)

Chameleon shrimp

Chameleon shrimp are available in rock pools and vary greatly in colour because, as their name suggests, they can change colour. This is done by eating differently coloured algae. They are up to 2.5cm (1in) long and are a good source of food, but collection takes time. Find a good sized rock pool and sweep your fine net through the algae and you will come up with one or two of these shrimp. Their great advantage is that they are available throughout the year.

Copepods

Copepods are very small crustaceans that live among the plankton. In an established marine tank you will find various species of copepods. They are usually the first thing you notice as you turn the lights on, as they are usually on the glass. They disappear into the gravel at the bottom of the tank as soon as the light comes on. They are ideal fry food, but very difficult to produce in large numbers.

Dead food

Some seahorses will accept dead food after being trained to do so. This can be a long process, some taking up to eight weeks to accept it. If you can persuade them to take dead food this is very useful for short periods of time. However, it should not be used full time, as the nutritional content of dead food is far too low to give them a balanced diet. In the process of thawing out dead food 50% of the nutritional value is lost, which causes problems for an animal with very high nutritional needs.

River shrimp

These are similar to mysis and are occasionally available in pet shops. However, they are very expensive and their availability is irregular.

Mysis shrimp

If you do not have access to a daily supply of mysis, consider carefully whether or not you are in a position to keep seahorses, as live mysis shrimp are their most important food. These shrimp are about 2cm (0.75in) long and semi-transparent. Adult seahorses eat 30 to 40 shrimp a day, so these should always be available. However, you cannot buy them, and have to fish for them every day, summer and winter. In summer months they are present in large numbers, but in winter they sink to the bottom of the estuaries where they live and are almost impossible to find.

It takes time and experience to locate the best sites for them, which are usually found on the opposite side to the tidal current. This means that, if the tide is coming in, they are on the 'up' side of an object in the water; if the tide is going out, they are on the 'down' side of the current. This is how they shelter from the full force of the tidal pull. Sweep a long-handled fine net through the surface of the water - if the mysis are there they will be caught in the net. Transfer the shrimp into a bucket full of the estuary water. If you have a long journey, use a battery powered air pump and air line or the shrimp will die of lack of oxygen. Before feeding the shrimp to the seahorses, rinse them under a running tap to make sure they are as clean as possible.

Rockhoppers and side swimmers

These again are a good source of food but slow to collect. They look similar to land-based woodlice but are found in rock pools under the rocks. Turn over the rocks and quickly sweep the area with your net. You will come up with myriad small crustacea, side swimmers among them. Always remember to turn the rock the right way up again when you have finished.

Side swimmer

Rockhopper

Rotifers

A very useful rearing animal for seahorse fry, rotifers are about 1mm across. They are available from tropical fish outlets and you can propagate them for yourself using the same method as for brine shrimp (see page 16). You can feed the rotifers on baker's yeast but enrich them in the same way as brine shrimp before you give them to the fry. You need a large number of pots of rotifers on the go at the same time because they are not as prolific as brine shrimp.

Guppy fry and mollie fry

The fry of guppies and mollies are a good source of food but not all species of seahorses will take them, especially the smaller species.

*I*ndex

Big Bellied Seahorse 18, 20, 39

guttulatus 23, 34, 37

Black Seaponie 40

Brine shrimp 14, 16–17,
21–23, 46

Chameleon shrimp 46

Copepods 46

Dead food 16, 24, 40, 46

Fungus 27–29

Gas Bubble disease 27

Golden Seaponie 21, 38

Guppy fry 47

Hippocampus abdominalis 18, 20, 39

Hippocampus breviceps 41

Hippocampus comes 9, 29, 32

Hippocampus fuscus 40

Hippocampus hippocampus 37, 42

Hippocampus histrix 36

Hippocampus ingens 6

Hippocampus kuda 13–15, 30

Hippocampus 23, 34, 37,
42, 45

Hippocampus whitei 21, 38

Knobby Seahorse 41

Kuda Seahorse 13–15, 30

Mollie fry 47

Mysis shrimp 11, 15–16, 23, 47

Phyllopteryx taeniolatus 6, 8

Pipefish 5, 8

Prickly Seahorse 36

River shrimp 14, 46

Rockhoppers 14, 47

Rotifers 21, 47

Seadragon 6, 8

Short Snouted Seahorse 37, 42

Side swimmers 14, 47

Spiny Seahorse 23, 26, 34,
37, 42, 45

Tiger Tail Seahorse 9, 29, 32

Yellow Philippine
(*Hippocampus sp*) 26

Seahorses are among the most beautiful and
enchanting of marine fish.
Unless you can provide all their needs, in
particular paying attention to their food
requirements, then please
<u>DO NOT</u>
attempt to keep them.
They will only suffer needlessly and will die.

Printed in Hong Kong through Printworks Int. Ltd.